Sew Celtic

designed and written by
NIKKI FOLEY

Nikki Foley

Published in 2012 by Nikki Foley

Sew Celtic by Nikki Foley
Photography by Nikki Foley
Illustrations by Olly Foley & Fergus Cronin
Graphic design by iDesign

Printed In Ireland.

Sew
Celtic

The Sewing Shed 'The Cutest Little Quilt Shop in Ireland'
Ballyarkane
Keel
Castlemaine
Co Kerry
Ireland

www.thesewingshed.com
info@thesewingshed.ie

Thank you to:

Kerry Bog Village 18th century village on the ring of Kerry,
for use of their facilities http://www.kerrybogvillage.ie

Romi Buhles who long arm quilted Bog Cabin and Shades of green so beautifully.

Karen Farrell for help with the sewing and proof reading.

To my beautiful Mum who guided me to where I am now.

To everyone else who supported me and believed in me – you know who you are.

Bog Village in County Kerry

Contents

Page 12
Page 38
Page 42
Page 34
Page 9
Page 22
Page 16
Page 5
Page 19
Page 28
Page 31
Page 25

Forward

There are some combinations that just seem to be destined for each other..... ice cream and hot chocolate sauce, bluebells and beech woods, Brad and Angelina to name a few. Well here is one more. Kerry scenery and lovely quilts! I fell in love with Kerry as a child spending every holiday running free through fields, climbing mountains and jumping from rock to rock in rivers and on beaches with my cousins, in what has easily to be one of the most beautiful places on earth. The photographs in this book stir so many great memories.

Then, over 30 years ago I was doubly lucky to discover quilts and quilting, (an instant addiction for which I have ever since been actively fighting a cure!) So to discover quilters in Kerry who shared my passion completed the circle. They are indeed a blessed group, as just outside their doors lie vistas, colours, and ideas galore which, with the addition of a little Celtic magic can inspire beautiful quilts for today. Nikki's lovely projects in this book, spring from these roots, and will be a joy to make and enjoy in your home......... and if you have never been to Kerry may I suggest that you plan your visit as you sew.

Angela Madden.
Author, Textile Artist and Teacher.
Website www.angelamadden.com

County Kerry, Ireland

Introduction

A strength of mine is finding inspiration in most anything visual and most certainly, design comes from my own surroundings. Living in Ireland gives feeling and vision for my designs. It is the perfect place for inspiration. The Irish colours of nature stay fresh and vivid with many thanks to our island's never-ending flow of rainfall.

Stepping back into time, the history of Ireland sparks passion and inspiration in me and my designs. Irish mythology is a fascinating subject and has become my muse. Imagine, people in ancient times storytelling around the fire. Illustrious tales of Celtic warriors and mythical characters create the folklore that makes Ireland so special. In this book, these elements are found in projects based on ancient mythical tales.

Sewing, of course, is a large part of my life. Located on Dingle Peninsula, The Sewing Shed is where I share, teach and sell all things patchwork since opening the shop several years ago. The West Coast of Ireland, overlooking the Atlantic Ocean and with Kerry mountains of green and purple is a wonderful place for designing and creating. Each day I breathe in the fresh air, gaze out at the sea while sheep graze in the green fields below. Idyllic, and now captured for you in this book.

For obvious reasons, another interest of mine is photography and I'm happy to share with you all my own photographs seen in this book. Now you know what inspires me, I hope the projects in this book encourage and motivate you to create and sew.

Happy Sewing,

Nikki Foley

The Sewing Shed
Ballyarkane,
Keel,
Castlemaine,
County Kerry,
Ireland.

www.thesewingshed.com
info@thesewingshed.ie

About Nikki

From a young age Nikki Foley has had a love of colour and design. Studying graphic design in college, Nikki honed her design skills but held uncertainty for her career path. Shortly after starting a young family, Nikki returned to higher education on a part-time basis. Now, mother to six boys, Nikki is proficient with certificates in A-level art, interior design, adult teaching, and City & Guilds patchwork and quilting. Nikki is a firm believer in continued education and is currently studying judicial competency accredited through the Quilters Guild of the British Isles.

Drawn to fabric and beautiful colours, Nikki found her love for patchwork 19 years ago with English paper piecing. Excelling in a variety of techniques, Nikki cultivated her patchwork abilities and talent into professional designs and patterns. Nikki's work was featured throughout the Quick Quilts series by Rosemary Wilkinson. Upbeat and sociable, Nikki has always found time away from designing to teach and share patchwork with students of all levels in person and online.

Nikki offers a wide variety of talks and workshops on textile art, patchwork and quilting.

Originally from Birmingham England, Nikki married an Irish man, and with their six sons, they relocated to his homeland of County Kerry in 2003. Soon after, Nikki opened her own patchwork shop, The Sewing Shed, where new friends, patterns and interests are ever evolving. From its picturesque location on the road to Dingle, Nikki's shop is a busy hub of patchwork. Beyond teaching and selling, Nikki organises exhibitions, hosts tour groups and leads local quilting bees.

Recently, her published work can be found in a variety of magazines as Nikki is a regular contributor to Irish Quilting and other publications such as Fabrications and British Patchwork and quilting. In 2007, Nikki was credited with founding the southwest branch of the Irish Patchwork Society (IPS) and served as Chairperson in 2008-2010. She is still active in the southwest IPS branch serving more than 25 patchwork members in the Kerry area.

Dingle, Ireland

Before You Start

Templates are at the back of the book.

Read the instructions through first, this will give you a better understanding of the project.

Use a ¼ inch seam allowance and press seams as you go.

- Place the fusible webbing paper side up over the pattern pieces.

- "Trace" each pattern piece the required number of times.

- Remember that a reverse image results from all the traced pieces. For symmetrical pieces this is not a problem. For other images, turn the pattern sheet over and trace the design from the other side of the sheet (unless the pattern designer has already reversed the images). This will give a reverse image that will revert once ironed onto the fabric and cut out.

- Once pieces are traced onto the fusible webbing, "roughly cut" around each shape. Do not cut on the drawn line!

- Using a medium heat dry iron, press the fusible webbing (paper side up) onto the wrong side of your chosen fabrics.

- Using small sharp scissors cut out the shape exactly on the drawn line. Take care when handling the fabric to avoid fraying the edges.

- Peel the paper backing from the pattern piece. A fine layer of adhesive will remain on the fabric.

- Using the picture as a guide, place the pieces into position onto the background fabric, and use a medium heat iron to bond in place.

- Use your preferred method of stitching to stitch around your appliqué pieces.

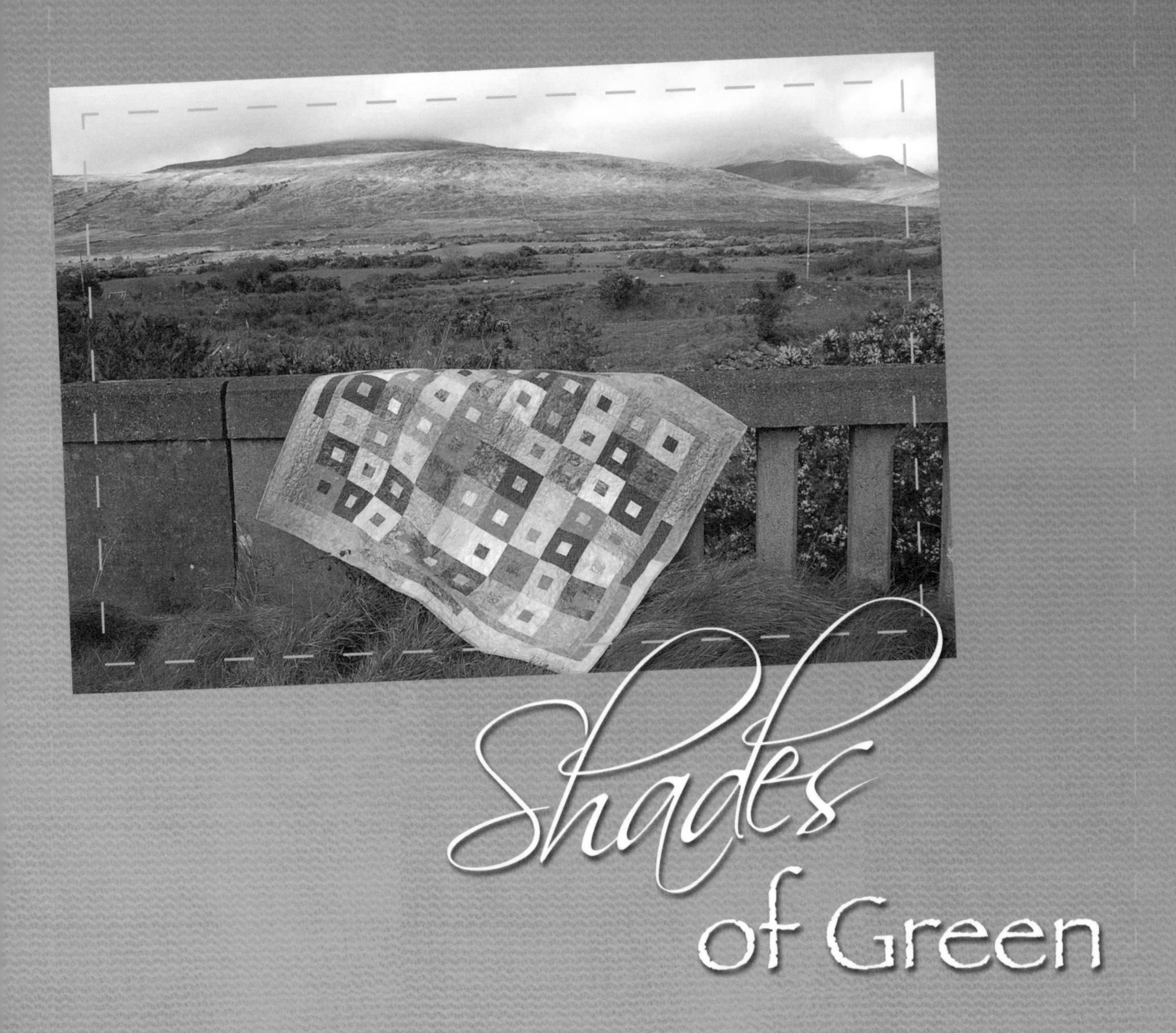

Shades of Green

As the rain clears and the colours begin to emerge...
...endless shades of green

Shades of Green

Finished size 64 ½ x 75 ½ inches

Ireland is truly every shade of green you can imagine. I love the depth of the colour, and sometimes when I look out the window as the rain clears and the colours begin to emerge, I try and count the different shades. I'm never sure of how far I get as I always get distracted by something else just as beautiful on the landscape.
Look at the effect of all the divided fields, and they look like quilts already, so this quilt is based on the endless shades of green that can be viewed all year round.

I hope you enjoy collecting all the different shades of green; this can be challenging but fun. You can use as many as you like, this one was made with a total of 15 colours.

Requirements:

- 10 inches from 14 different shades of green fabric
- 12 inches of olive green fabric
- 16 Inches of jade green for binding
- Wadding and backing to fit

From experience:

When choosing the fabrics, go for a mix of light, medium and dark greens but with a higher ratio of medium and dark.

Cutting:

Cut the fourteen 10 inch wide green fabrics into 2 ½ inch strips across the width of fabric. There will be 56 strips in total. The rest of the cutting will be done as you go.

Border 1 - from the olive green fabric cut six 2 inch strips across the width of fabric

Binding: Cut eight 2 ½ inch strips across the width of fabric.

Sewing

Use a ¼ inch seam allowance and press seams as you go.

The instructions are for one block. It is easier to do some of the cutting as you go, to enable you the best use of the fabric

Choose a green fabric strip and from this cut a 2 ½ inch centre square.
Choose a different green 2 ½ inch strip of fabric, from this strip cut:
 Two 2 ½ inch squares
 Two pieces 6 ½ inches.

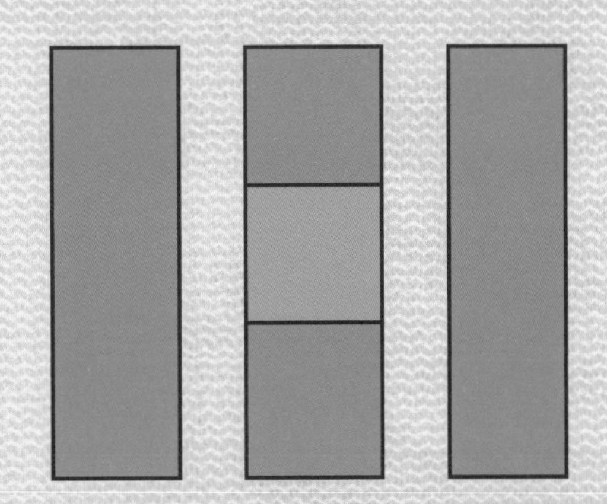

Sew the 2 ½ inch squares to the top and bottom of the centre square.

Sew a 6 ½ inch strip to either side

The measurement of the block is 6 ½ inches (finished size 6 inches)

Repeat the above instructions with 55 centre squares.

Layout the blocks into 9 rows of 7, refer to the picture for guidance.
Sew each row of blocks together, and then sew the rows together.

Border 1
Join and cut the 2 inch wide olive green strips to the following measurements
Two border strips 42 ½ inches
Two border strips 56 ½ inches

Pin and sew the 42 ½ inch long borders to the top and bottom of the quilt. Sew the remaining two borders to either side of the quilt.

Use the remaining 2 ½ inch mixed green strips both full length and left overs to create the two rounds of borders. Use different colours within each border. Join, cut and sew to the following measurements below.

Border 2
Two border strips 45 ½ inches
Two border strips 64 ½ inches

Pin and sew the 45 ½ inch borders to the top and bottom of the quilt. Sew the remaining two to either side of the quilt

Border 3
Make in the same way as border 2 to the following measurments below.

Two border strips 49 ½ inches
Two border strips 65 ½ inches

Pin and sew the 49 ½ inch borders to the top and bottom of the quilt. Sew the remaining two borders to either side of the quilt.

Sew the binding strips into one continuous length and refer to page 45 for finishing instructions.

Farmhouse Blue

A jug of milk straight from the cow
with a thick band of cream on top

Farmhouse Blue

Finished size 34 x 34 inches

I always feel inspired by colours I have encountered in Ireland. Not just from the landscape but from everyday living, on this occasion my colours came from the simple living of farmhouse life.
Years ago, my husband used to take me to visit his very good friends, who had a farm and kept cows. I loved the warm and friendly smile of Ann when we arrived. At the kitchen table a jug of milk straight from the cow with a thick band of cream on top, was placed on the table. The cup of tea never tasted so good. For me it was not just the tea, but the hospitality, warmth and love in the house.

Requirements:

- 36 x 36 inches of 1 inch grid fusible webbing
- 18 inches of Navy fabric
- Fat quarter of mid blue fabric
- Fat quarter of Light blue fabric
- 28 inches Cream fabric
- Water soluble pen
- Wadding and backing to fit

Cutting:

The pattern in the centre of this quilt is called trip around the world.
For the centre and nine patch corner blocks:-

From the navy fabric cut:
68 - 2 inch squares

From the mid blue fabric cut:
56 - 2 inch squares

From the light blue fabric cut:
60 - 2 inch squares

From the cream fabric cut:
68 - 2 inch squares.

Borders

Border 1:
Cut 2 navy border strips 1 ½ x 22 ½ inches and 2 border strips 1 ½ x 20 strips

Border 2:
Cut 4 cream strips 5 x 24 ½ inches

From the remaining navy fabric cut 4 strips across the width of the fabric 2 ½ inches wide for the binding.

Fusible grid:

Cut the fusible grid into one piece 30x30 inches
From the remaining fusible grid cut 4 squares 6 x6 inches.

Farmhouse Blue

Instructions

Use a ¼ inch seam allowance. Press seams as you go.
If you received instructions with your fusible grid, read through them first.
Please note: Layout the fusible webbing on a surface near to your iron.

Following the picture below, place the 2 inch squares onto the fusible side of the grid. One fabric square will cover four 1 inch squares on the grid. When you are happy that all the squares are placed evenly on the grid, iron in place.

Starting on any side of the fused squares-Fold over the first line of squares so they are face to face with the second line. Sew along the edge using a ¼ inch seam allowance. Repeat with the next line until you have sewn all the lines, across the piece.
Turn the piece over so the back is facing up. Use a small sharp pair of scissors to cut along the fold of the fusible grid along each line. Take care not to cut the fabric of the squares. Iron open on each line.
Sew the lines of the grid the other way. Start by folding over the first line of squares with the second line, and sew along the edge. Continue until you have completed each line.

Repeat the above method to make the nine patch blocks, using the 6x6 inch fusible grid. Make four exactly the same.

Borders

Sew a navy border strip 1 ½ x 22 ½ inches to the top and bottom of the centre piece. Then sew the remaining two borders to either side and press.

Sew a cream 5 inch x 24 ½ inch strip to the top and bottom of the centre piece.

Refer to the picture on the left and sew a nine patch block to each end of the remaining two cream 5 x 24 ½ inch cream borders. Matching up the corners, sew onto either side of the centre piece.

Celtic band on the cream border.

Find the centre point of each cream border, by folding the quilt top in half. Finger crease the centre point on the border.
Place the Celtic band template, underneath the cream fabric. Pin in place and using the water soluble pen, trace the design onto the fabric. Do this on each border.

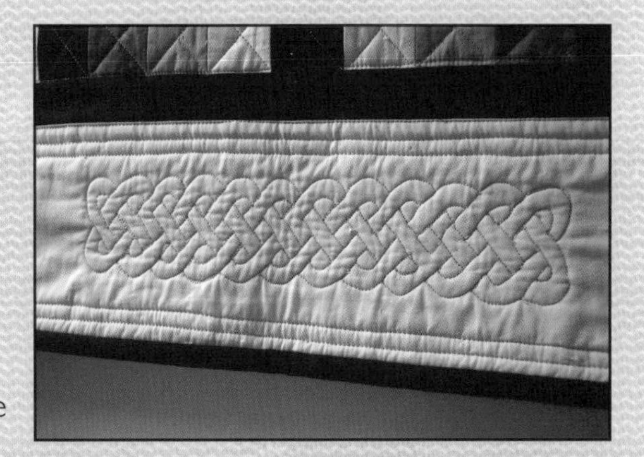

Layer up the quilt with wadding and backing and pin and tack. Follow instructions on page 45 for further details

Quilt through the centre square's diagonally both ways using a walking foot on your sewing machine. Do the same with the outer nine patch blocks.

Use free motion stitching to quilt along the lines of the Celtic band on the cream border. Use a light thread if you are worried about getting the lines straight. If you are confident use a light blue thread. Alternatively you could hand quilt the Celtic band.

Join the binding into a continuous length and follow the finishing instructions on page 45.

Bog Cabin

A turf fire must be the scent of Ireland

Bog Cabin

Finished size 71 ½ x 79 ½ inches

Green is the colour of Ireland, and a soft day the touch, bacon and cabbage the taste, and harp music the sound, then a turf fire must be the scent of Ireland. This quilt was inspired by the colours of the bog, where the turf is gathered. The dark dramatic hues of rich brown, tan with hints of purple and green are a great combination to recreate the colours of the bog. Make this soft but dramatic quilt to recreate your own bog quilt.

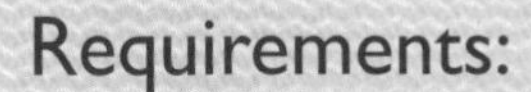

Requirements:

- 4 yards of rich brown fabric
- 40 inches of purple fabric
- ½ yard of rust fabric
- ½ yard of gold fabric
- ½ yard of olive green fabric
- ½ yard of light green fabric

Cutting:

From the rich brown fabric cut:
24 strips measuring 2 ½ inches across the width of fabric, from these strips cut the following sections:
Twenty four- 4 ½ inch
Forty eight- 6 ½ inch
Forty eight -10 ½ inch
Cut 7 strips measuring 10 inches across the width of the fabric for the outer border

From EACH of the rust, gold, olive green and purple fabric cut the following sections:
Twelve – 2 ½ x 4 ½ inch
Twelve – 2 ½ x 8 ½ inch

From the remaining purple fabric cut eight 2 ½ inch strips across the width of fabric for the binding.

From the light green fabric cut seven 2 ½ inch strips across the width of the fabric.

Bog Cabin

Sewing

Please note: The olive green and rust blocks are sewn in a different direction to the purple and gold. Read instructions through first so you get a full understanding.
Use a ¼ inch seam allowance throughout and press seams as you go.
Block size 10 ½ x 12 ½ inches (finished 10x12)

Rust and brown bog cabin block

Follow diagram below and work in an anti clockwise direction. The instructions are for one block.

- Sew a brown 4 ½ inch section to a rust 4 ½ inch section lengthways together.
- Keep the brown section at the top, and sew a rust 4 ½ inch section to the right hand side.
- Sew a brown 6 ½ section to the top
- Sew a brown 6 ½ inch section to the left hand side
- Sew a rust 8 ½ inch to the bottom
- Sew a rust 8 ½ inch section to the right hand side
- Sew a brown 10 ½ inch section to the top
- Sew a brown 10 ½ inch section to the left hand side

Make 6 of these blocks.

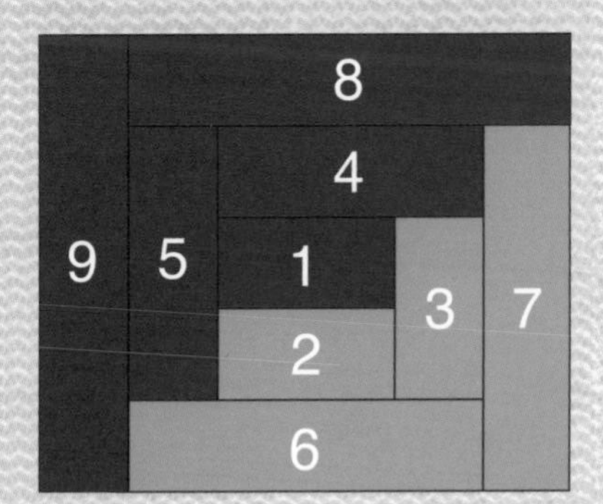

Olive green and brown bog cabin block

Repeat the above instructions replace the rust fabric with the olive green fabric
Make 6 of these blocks.

Purple and brown bog cabin block

Follow the picture below and work in a clockwise direction. The instructions are for one block.

- Sew a brown 4 ½ inch section to purple 4 ½ inch section lengthways together.
- Keep the brown section at the top, and sew a purple 4 ½ inch section to the left hand side.
- Sew a brown 6 ½ inch section to the top
- Sew a brown 6 ½ inch section to the right hand side
- Sew a purple 8 ½ inch section to the bottom
- Sew a purple 8 ½ inch section to the left hand side
- Sew a brown 10 ½ inch section to the top
- Sew a brown 10 ½ inch section to the right hand side

Make 6 of these blocks.

Gold and brown bog cabin block
Repeat the previous instructions, replace the purple fabric with the gold fabric.
Make 6 of these blocks.

Sew a rust, olive green, purple and gold bog cabin block together. Sew in pairs then sew the pairs together Repeat this with the remaining blocks. You will have six large blocks measuring 24 ½ x 20 ½ inches.

Refer to the picture of the quilt and layout the large blocks. Sew them together in rows then sew the rows together. This makes up the quilt centre and should measure 48 ½ x 60 ½ inches.

Adding borders
If your quilt centre is a different measurement to above, then adjust your borders to fit.

Join the light green border strips into a continuous length, cut the following borders from this length:
Two borders 48 ½ inches
Two borders 64 ½ inches

Sew the 48 ½ inch borders onto the top and bottom of the quilt centre. Then sew the 64 ½ inch borders to either side of the quilt centre.
Measurement of quilt top with border 1 – 52 ½ x 64 ½ inches.

Join the brown border strips into a continuous length, cut the following borders from this length:
Two borders 52 ½ inches
Two borders 79 ½ inches

Sew the 52 ½ inch borders onto the top and bottom of the quilt centre. Then sew the 79 ½ inch borders to either side of the quilt centre. Finished quilt size 71 ½ x 79 ½ inches.

Binding- Join the eight 2 ½ inch wide binding strips together into a continuous length and refer to page 45 & 46 for finishing instructions.

Patchwork Fields are Green

Endless fields create a patchwork of nature

Patchwork Fields are Green

Finished size 17 x 20 inches

The pattern supplied for this in the templates section is reduced, please enlarge by 150 per cent or to required size. The pattern looks great in any size.

Requirements:

- Freezer paper
- Flat head flower pins
- ½ yard black
- 6/7 scraps or fat 8th of green fabrics.
- Scrap or fat 8th of sky
- Scrap of white
- Thread for quilting.
- Wadding and backing to fit

Place a piece of freezer paper over the master copy, shiny side down. Trace the pattern design onto the paper side. Add the numbers and registration marks to the freezer paper copy.

Cut out the oval from the freezer paper, make only one cut in from the side as you need to keep the outer piece, which you can now roll up and keep for later. From the oval freezer paper pattern , cut out pieces numbered 1 and 2
Iron each piece, shiny side down onto the right side of the chosen fabrics. Cut out allowing a ¼ inch seam allowance around each piece.
With the freezer paper still on the fabric, place the first two pieces together face to face. Using flat head flower pins, pin from the centre, line up the registration marks as you go. Use plenty of pins to achieve accuracy. Clip any extreme curves. Sew from one edge to the other, using the edge of freezer paper as a guide, but try not to catch the freezer paper in the stitching. Continue with the rest of the pieces. Sew together in number order to complete the centre. Choose fabrics carefully and put in appropriate place, refer to the picture as a guide.

Remove the freezer paper and press seams to one side.

From the black fabric cut in half through the centre to give you 2 pieces measuring approx 18x 22inches.
(you now have 2 fat quarters)

From one of these pieces cut a window:- To cut the window find the centre of the black fat ¼. Place the outer piece of the freezer paper over the fat quarter shiny side down, try and place the centre of the oval over the centre of the fat quarter. Iron in place. Cut the fabric ½ inch away from the line on the inside of the freezer paper; take your time to ensure curve of the oval is correct.

Keep the cut out piece of black from the centre. Leave the freezer paper in place. Clip the curves around the whole oval, each cut should be at a right angle to the edge and 1/8th inch deep. Press the seam allowance to the back, just beyond the cuts in the fabric. Use the edge of the freezer paper to guide you. Remove the freezer paper.

Place the window over the pieced landscape, pin to the landscape at the top, bottom and at both sides. Then pin in-between the gaps to secure the whole piece. Then tack around the edge by hand, to secure the layers, then sew on machine with black thread.

Sheep - Add tiny oval pieces of white fabric to the fields and stitch in place. Use a fabric pen to draw legs and head.

Appliqué the shamrocks

Trace the shamrock shapes and the leaves onto the paper side of fusible webbing. Iron onto shamrock coloured fabric remove paper backing, iron in place on the landscape and stitch in place.
Alternatively you can make 3 d shamrocks :- Iron a piece of green fabric to a piece of fusible webbing, remove the paper from the webbing, iron another piece of green fabric to the back, so the fusible webbing is sandwiched between the two fabrics. The right sides of both of the fabrics should be facing outwards.

Make a template, by tracing and cutting out the shamrock from the template section. Stick it on to card and cut out.
Draw around the template, onto the green bonded fabrics, do this for as many shamrocks as you wish. Sew the shamrocks to the finished piece, either by machine or by hand.

Now use the cut out black fabric oval as a pattern to cut a piece of wadding, place on top of the wadding and cut ½ inch larger than the oval. Place this piece of wadding behind the pieced landscape and pin in place from the front.
Square to 17 x 20 inches.
From the remaining fat quarter of black, cut five 2 ½ inch strips and join together into a continuous length. Refer to page 45 For finishing instructions.

Tip:

Quilt a straight line approx 1/8th of inch away from the line of the oval on the black using black thread. You could free motion the black background or just continue with a straight stitch with your walking foot.

Shamrock Sue

Tending her sheep and enjoying her Shamrocks

Shamrock Sue

Finished size 39 ½ x 39 ½ inches

This is a fun quilt to make. Sun Bonnet sue is combined with traditional Irish chain block. She is tending her sheep and enjoying her Shamrocks.

Requirements:

- ½ yard of warm yellow fabric
- 20 inches of sage green fabric
- ½ yard of cream fabric
- ¾ yard of deep red fabric
- Scraps for applique
- Fusible Webbing

Cutting:

From the cream fabric cut:
Four 6 ½ inch squares
Sixteen 2 ½ x 6 ½ inch rectangles
Twenty 2 ½ inch squares

From the warm yellow fabric cut:
Seventy six 2 ½ inch squares

From the sage green fabric cut:
Forty five 2 ½ inch squares
Two border strips 3 x 34 ½ inches
Two border strips 3 x 39 ½ inches

From the deep red fabric cut:
Two border strips 2 ½ x 30 ½ inches
Two border strips 2 ½ x 34 ½ inches
Four 2 ½ inch strips across the width of fabric for the binding.

Sewing

Use a ¼ inch seam allowance and press all seams as you go.

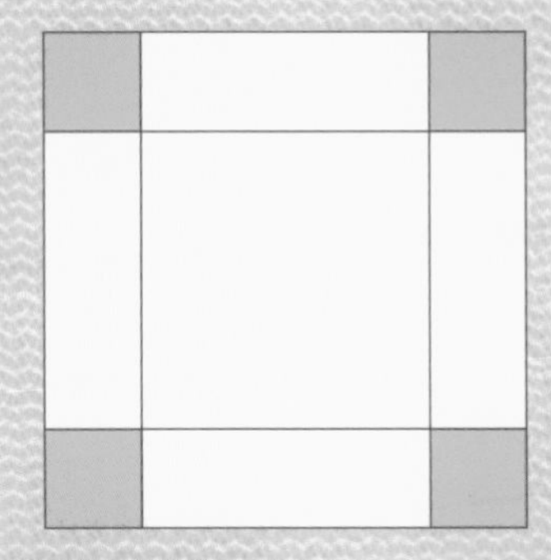

Refer to the diagram to make four blocks. The instructions are for one block.

Sew a cream 2 ½ x 6 ½ inch rectangle to the top and bottom of a cream 6 ½ inch square.
Sew a yellow 2 ½ inch square onto each end of a 2 ½ x 6 ½ inch rectangle. Repeat and sew to either side of the cream 6 ½ inch block.

Refer to the diagram to make five blocks . The instructions are for one block.

Lay out the 2 ½ inch squares as in the diagram. Sew together in rows. When you press the seams, alternate the direction in each row this will help the squares ' lock' together.

Applique

Trace the parts of sunbonnet sue four times, onto the paper side of fusible webbing. Repeat with two sheep, three hearts, six shamrocks and a watering can. Cut each shape out roughly. Iron each one onto your chosen fabric. Cut out on drawn line, remove paper backing.

Work with one block at a time and lay out the pieces to build up the picture. When you are happy with the arrangement press in place. You can stitch around the appliqué pieces, either by hand using blanket stitch or on the machine. You may have a blanket stitch on your machine, or you can use a small zigzag stitch set close together.

Sew together the blocks and borders

Refer to the photo and lay out the blocks. Sew together in rows, and then sew the rows together.
Border 1:
Sew a deep red border strip 2 ½ x 30 ½ inches to the top and bottom of the quilt top .
Sew a deep red border strip 2 ½ x 34 ½ inches to either side.
Border 2:
Sew a sage green border strip 3 x 34 ½ inches to top and bottom of the quilt top.
Sew a sage green bordrer strip 3 x 39 ½ inches to either side.

Sew the deep red binding strips into a continuous length and refer to page 45 for finishing instructions.

I Love Ewe

Sheep will make you smile every day

I Love Ewe

Finished size 16 x 16 inches

These cute little sheep will make you smile every day when hung on your wall. Make it from small scraps for a real country feel, or use a coordinated fabric bundle that you can purchase ready selected in any quilt shop.

Requirements:

- Fat quarter of cream, pink, green, mustard, rust and brown.
- Two strips measuring 2 ½ x width of the fabric for the binding.
- Wadding and backing to fit.
- ¼ yard of fusible webbing.

Cutting:

From the cream fat quarter cut:
Five 5 ½ inch squares.

From each of the rust and pink fat quarters cut:
Five strips 1 ½ x 5 ½ inches.

From the mustard fat quarter cut:
Six strips 1 ½ x 5 ½ inches.

From the longest side of the green fat quarter cut:
Four 2 ½ inch strips for the binding.
Twelve squares 1 ½ x 1 ½ inches.
One green 7 ½ inch square, cut this diagonally both ways.

From the brown fat quarter cut;
Four squares 5 ½ x 5 ½ inches.
Cut in half diagonally once.

Sewing

Use a ¼ inch seam allowance and press seams as you go.

There are five sheep blocks, for each block trace onto the paper side of the fusible webbing:-
A sheep, pair of legs, head and a heart. Cut out each piece roughly.
Choose the fabric for each block. Use a selection of the pink, mustard, rust for the sheep bodies and hearts. Keep all the heads and legs brown. Iron the fusible pieces onto the chosen fabrics. Cut out on the drawn line. Remove paper backing and place the pieces on to the cream 5 ½ inch squares.
When you are happy with the placement iron the pieces in place. Blanket stitch to applique the pieces.

Follow the diagram below to sew the pieces together.

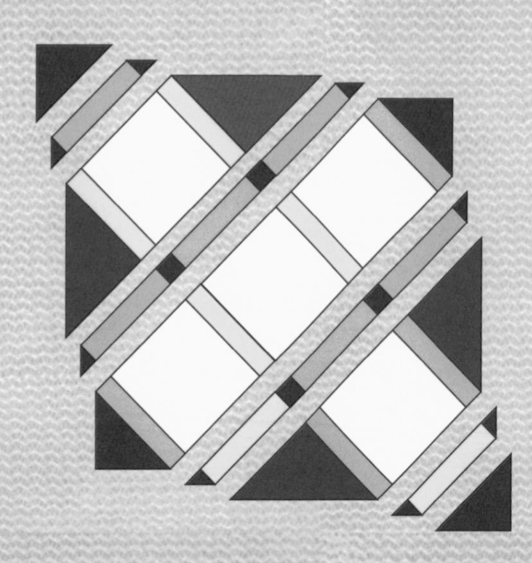

Sew together in rows.
Sew together the rows.
Square the piece to 16 ½ x 16 ½.

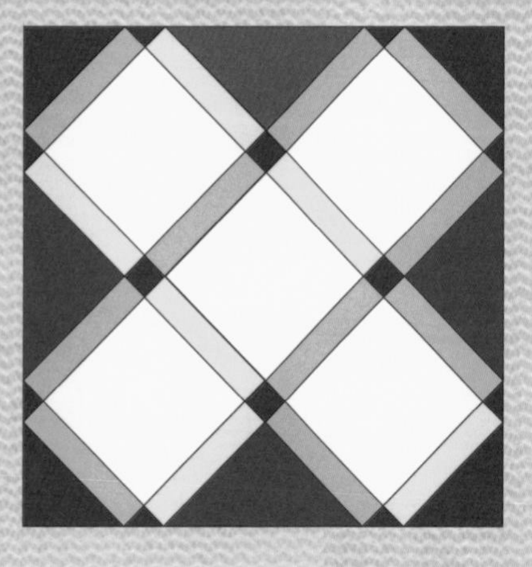

Join the binding strips together and refer to the finishing instructions on page 45.

St. Patricks Day Mug Mat

Sit back and enjoy your St. Patricks day

St. Patrick's Day Mug Mats

Finished size 9 x 13 inches

The perfect St Patricks day gift! Shamrock mug mats. Quick to make and ideal to sit your mug and biscuits on while you sit back and enjoy your St. Patricks day treat. Make with a selection of green fabrics.

Requirements:

- Foundation fabric calico or muslin 13 x 10 inches
- Scraps of greens approx. 3 ½ x 3 ½ inches
- Fat quarter of dark green fabric
- 3 inch x 26 inch of bright green fabric
- Two 2 ½ inch strips across the width of dark green fabric

Cutting:

Cut up the scraps of green into approx ten 3 ½ inch x varying widths of 1 ½ - 2 ½ inches.
From the dark green fabric cut:
Two strips 13 x 2 ½ inches.
From the bright green fabric cut:
Two pieces 3 x 13 inches

St. Patrick's Day Mug Mats

Sewing

Sew all the pieces together measuring 3 ½ inch wide into one long piece. Sew them in a random order, the final length should be 13 inches. Place onto the centre of the foundation fabric lengthways, pin in place Lay the 3 x 13 inch bright green fabric strips either side of the centre panel, so the raw edges are butted against each other. Pin in place.

Cut the first dark green strip measuring 2 ½ x 13 inches in half lengthways using a wavy line. Repeat with the second dark green strip. Lay the strips on top of the table runner use the photograph for placement. Pin in place.

Quilt as you go

Layer up with wadding and backing. Pin and tack the layers together For further instructions refer to page 45.
Quilting suggestion - Quilt along the dark fabrics, meander with the walking foot and a straight stitch to create wavy lines. Use a sparkly thread or variegated thread in shades of green.
You will need to quilt approx. 1 inch apart, to hold the fabric layers down. Keep the quilting on the dark fabrics only.

Applique

On the paper side of fusible webbing trace small shamrocks. Cut each one out roughly. Iron onto the reverse of your chosen fabrics. Cut out on the drawn line, remove the paper backing. Place the shamrocks onto the table runner. When you are happy with the placement, iron in place to fuse.
Use a decorative stitch, or zig zag on your machine to applique the shamrocks.
Square and trim to 9 x 13 inches

Join the binding strips together and follow finishing instructions on page 45.

The Atlantic Ocean from the Coast of Ireland

Shamrocks

Celebrate your Irish roots

Finished size 22 x 25 inches

If you ask anyone what they associate with Ireland then they will most probably say 'shamrocks'.

Make this wall hanging to celebrate your Irish roots, or maybe as a gift for someone who lives away from home.

Requirements:

- 1 yard of plain black fabric
- 3 / 4 fat quarters in different shades of green
- Wadding and backing 22x25 inches
- Fabric glue

Shamrock templates - Make a template by tracing the small shamrock onto paper. Stick the paper to card, and cut out. Repeat with the large shamrock template.

Cutting:

From the black:
Cut a rectangle centre piece 17 x 20 inches.
Cut four border strips 2 x 22 inches
For the binding cut three 2 ½ inch strips across the width of the fabric

From a green fat quarter:
Cut two border strips 1 ½ x 20 inches
Cut two border strips 1 ½ x 19 inches

From the remaining green fat quarters:
Place the large shamrock template onto the fabric- trace around using a pencil or other marking tool. Cut out on drawn line. Repeat so you have 4 large shamrocks in total. Use a different fabric for each one.
Repeat using the small shamrock template to trace and cut out 20 shamrocks using a selection of all the green fabrics.

Sewing

Sew a green border 1 ½ x 20 inches to each side of the black centre piece.
Sew a green border 1 ½ x 19 inches to the top and bottom of the black centre

Sew a black border 2 x 22 inches to either side of the centre piece
Sew a black border 2 x 22 inches to top and bottom of the centre piece

Placement of shamrocks

Using the picture as a guide place the shamrocks onto the black 17 x 20 inch centre
There is one row of four large shamrocks
There are four rows of five shamrocks

When you are happy with the placements of the shamrock's, using the fabric glue pen, put a small amount of glue on the back of each one and press down in place. The glue will hold the shamrocks in place while you stitch them.

Layer up the top with wadding and backing – see finishing instructions on page 45.
Pin and tack the layers together.

Raw Edge Applique

On a small wall hanging like this it is possible to applique your pieces while quilting at the same time. Using a green thread , free motion around the edge of each shamrock. Go around each shape at least twice. Repeat until each shamrock is stitched down.
Alternatively use a small zig zag stitch on your machine.

Using black thread quilt the background and border.
Do not quilt the green border. This will make it stand out.

Join the binding into one continuous strip and follow the instructions for finishing on page 45.

Traditional Irish iron roof cottage

The Selkie Sea

Sad romantic tales of seals who take on human form.

The Selkie Sea

Finished size 27 x 31 inches

I love the tales of Irish folk lore and mythology. The story of the Selkies always intrigues me.

Selkies are seals who can shed their skin on land and take on human form. They can put the skin back on and return to the sea but cannot return to land for 7 years. Many stories of Selkies are sad romance tales, which the female Selkie leaves her human partner for the sea. The reputation of the male Selkie is rather more seductive, waiting on the shore for lonely fisherman's wives, with a mind to seduce them with their mystical powers.

This wall hanging is based on Selkies and the sea they swim in.
Most of the of the fabrics in this project are hand dyed, you can use batiks instead for a similar effect. The quilt is made with free style applique. Experiment with the applique shapes, try different placements and play with the arrangement to create your own Selkie sea piece.

Requirements:

- Pale blue Centre square 18 x 22 inches
- 20 inches of turquoise blue/pink fabric across the width
- Assortment of scraps white, light purple, dark purple, pink turquoise blue, sea green etc.
- Small piece of sand coloured fabric for seals
- 1 yard of fusible webbing
- ¼ yard of purple fabric

Cutting:

From the turquoise blue / pink fabric cut:

- Two borders 5 x 22 inches
- Two borders 5 x 27 inches

From the purple fabric cut:

- Three 2 ½ inch strips across the width of the fabric for the binding.

Sewing
Use a ¼ inch seam allowance and press seams as you go.

To each side of the centre, sew a 5 x 22 inch border.
To the top and bottom of the centre sew a 5x 27 inch border.

Applique
Using the templates on page 55 & 56. Draw spirals, wedges, swirls etc. on to the paper side of fusible webbing, trace enough to cover the borders. Cut each shape out roughly and iron onto the reverse of the pink and purple fabrics. Cut out on drawn line and remove paper backing.

Again using the templates draw enough shapes for the centre, including the waves and seals heads. The waves should be white, and seals from a sand coloured fabric.

Place all your applique shapes, glue side down on to the background and when you are happy with the placement iron in place.

Layer up your quilt top with wadding and backing follow instructions on page 45 For further details.

Quilt as you go

Free Motion Stitching

Using a matching thread stitch on the very edge of each applique shape. Fill in the background with small and medium size swirls. Use a matching thread to the background fabric.

Using a fine tipped brown permanent marker, colour in the eyes and nose on the seals head. Add the detail to the seals head with different shades of light and dark sand coloured thread, stitch in whiskers with black thread.

Join the purple binding strips into a continuous length and follow instructions on page 45 for finishing.

The Kerry Coastline with the Macgillycuddy's Reeks as the back drop

Cú Chulain's Love Throw

When she met him, she fell as deeply in love
with him as he was with her

Cú Chulain's Love Throw

Finished size 43 X 43 inches

Fand is a faery queen, who was once married to the sea god Manannan. After he left her, she was preyed upon by three Fomorian warriors in a battle for control of the Irish Sea. Her only hope in winning the battle was to send for the hero Cú Chulain who would only agree to come, if she would marry him. She reluctantly acquiesced to his wishes, though when she met him, she fell as deeply in love with him as he was with her. Manannan who still cared for her, knew that the relationship between the human world and the world of the faery could not continue without eventually destroying the faeries. He erased the memory of one from the other by drawing his magical mantle between the two lovers. Fand was also a minor sea goddess who made her home both in the Otherworld and on the Islands of Man. With her sister, Liban, she was one of the twin goddesses of health and earthly pleasures. She was also known as "Pearl of Beauty". Some scholars believe she was a native Manx deity who was absorbed in the Irish mythology

Requirements:

- 1 strip of fabric 2 x 22 inches from 11 different colours. Purple, cerise pink, turquoise, orange, blue, pink, burgundy, lime green, orange, brown, black.
- 22 x 22inches of one inch fusible grid.
- Fat ¼ of mid sea green fabric.
- Fat ¼ of olive green fabric for the applique.
- 20 inches of deep sea green fabric.
- 21 inches across the width of fabric of purple fabric.
- ½ yard of rust coloured silk.
- ½ yard of fusible webbing.
- 5 yards or a roll of rainbow coloured fusible bias tape.
- Wadding and backing to fit.
- Transfer pencil.

Cutting:

Cut each of the 11 coloured fabric strips into 2 inch squares.
Cut the mid sea green fat quarter into a 17 ½ x 17 ½ inch square- cut in half diagonally both ways.
From the deep sea green fabric cut two squares 20 inches, cut in half diagonally once.
From the purple fabric: Cut two border strips 2 x 22 ½ inches, cut another two border strips 2 x 25 ½ inches.
Cut five strips across the width of fabric 2 ½ inches wide for the binding.
From the rust coloured silk, cut five 3 inch strips across the width of fabric

Sewing

Use a ¼ inch seam allowance and press seams as you go.

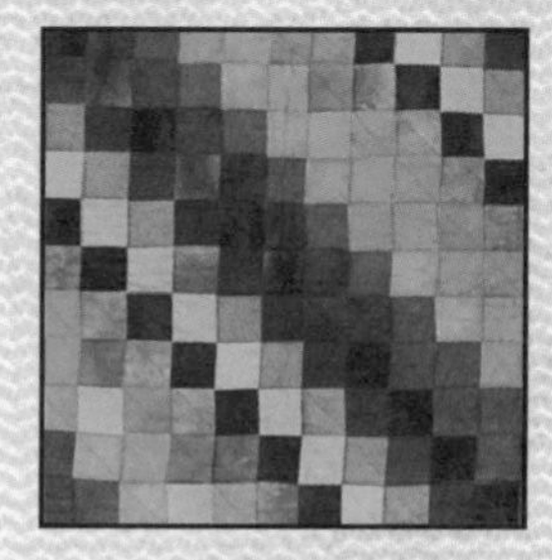

Read any instructions that come with your fusible grid before you start.

Place the 2 inch squares right sides up on the fusible grid, fusible side up. Use the diagram for placement of colours, each two inch square will cover four 1 inch squares on the grid.

When you are Happy that all the squares are placed evenly on the grid, iron in place.

Sewing

Starting on any side of the fused squares-Fold over the first line of squares so they are face to face with the second line. Sew along the edge using a ¼ inch seam allowance. Repeat with the next line until you have sewn all the lines, across the piece one way.
Turn the piece over so the back is facing up. Use a small sharp pair of scissors to cut along the fold of the fusible grid along each line. Take care not to cut the fabric of the squares. Iron open each line.
Sew the lines of the grid the other way. Start by folding over the first line of squares with the second line. And sew along the edge. Continue until you have completed each line. Cut along the fold of each line and iron open.

Sew the mid sea green triangles, taken from the 17 ½ x 17 ½ inch squares, to the centre square.
Stitch one to each side following the instructions below.
Match up the centre point of both edges by folding the long edge of the triangle in half and finger creasing. Also fold the edge of the centre, make a finger crease and match up the creases and pin from the centre out wards, before you sew.

Sew the remaining two triangles to the top and bottom.
Again find the centre point before you sew.

Applique

The applique is a series of swirls and Celtic shapes, you can make up your own creative arrangement using the templates on page 52 & 53. Or you can follow the picture of the quilt for placement.

Trace the shapes onto the paper side of fusible webbing. Cut each piece out roughly. Iron onto the reverse of the olive green fabric. Cut each shape out on the drawn line. Remove the paper backing and place onto the mid sea green fabric triangles. Look at picture for placement. Use a small zig zag on your machine with a matching thread to stitch along the edges of each piece.
Trim the piece to 22 ½ x 22 ½.

Sewing

Sew a purple 2 x 22 ½ inch border strip to either side of the centre. Sew a purple 2 x 25 ½ inch strip to the top and bottom of the centre.

Take two triangles cut from the deep sea green 20 inch squares. Sew to opposite sides of the centre. Match up the centre point of both edges by folding the long edge of the triangle in half and finger creasing. Also fold the edge of the centre, make a finger crease and match up the creases and pin from the centre out wards, before you sew. Repeat with the remaining two deep sea green triangles

Please note when sewing on the triangles, the long edge is on the bias, use lots of pins and make sure you do not stretch the fabric.

Square the quilt and trim to 38 inches.

Outer Border

Depending on the width of the silk, you may need to join the border strips so they are long enough.

Sew a 3 x 38 inch silk border strip to each side of the centre.
Sew a 3 x 43 inch silk border strip to the top and bottom of the centre.

Celtic Applique

Refer to the picture of the quilt for placement of the Celtic applique.

Celtic Knot Applique

You will need approx. 70 inches of ¼ inch bias tape for each Celtic knot. You can buy ready-made fusible bias, this is the easiest option.
If you wish to make your own you will need a bias making tool. Follow instructions to make ¼ inch bias tape. You will need extra fabric if you wish to make your own.
Trace the Celtic knot found on templates page 54 onto tracing paper with an iron-on transfer pencil. Centre and put the tracing paper in correct position - transfer side down, and use an iron on the wool setting to transfer the design onto your fabric. Work slowly and check to see if the design is transferring.

Start with the end of the bias tape on an intersection. Chose an under, so the raw edge will be covered when you cross back over it. Follow the design. Carefully note the location of the intersections, and whether the tape is to go under or over. Pin the bias tape to the background fabric. If you have fusible bias you can iron it in place as you go. As you complete your design, you can tuck the last piece which will meet the start, under the strip of bias that crosses over.

When you are happy with the placement. Use a invisible thread, or a matching thread to sew the bias in place. Sew a straight line down each side of the tape, turning the quilt slowly and smoothly on the curves of the bias. You could also use a decorative stitch, such as a blanket or zigzag stitch, or use twin needles: refer to your sewing machine manual for further details.

Complete all four Celtic knots.

Join the five purple 2 ½ inch border strips for the binding and follow instructions on page 45 for further details.

This quilt is perfect for embellishment.
Heat fix rhinestones were applied to this after the quilting was complete. If these are not available then beads or sequins could also be used to add an extra special effect.

Celtic Eternity

A good luck charm for longevity or a new beginning

Celtic Eternity

Finished size 56 x 56 inches

In history Celtic knots symbolised something very important, with no start and no end within the design, they were a good luck charm for longevity or a new beginning. They originated from the sign of the cross and if you look closely between the ribbons you can find crosses hidden within the design.

You could make this quilt with any group of colours for a breath-taking result.

Requirements:

- 2 yards of black or very dark purple
- ½ yard of green
- ½ yard of yellow
- ½ yard of blue
- ½ yard of blue swirls
- Iron on transfer pencil
- Bias tape – 5 yards of ready-made fusible bias tape in two colours to match your fabrics (10 yards in total)

Cutting:

From the black fabric cut:
Four 12 ½ inch squares
Five 4 ½ inch squares
Eighty 2 ½ inch squares
Six 2 ½ inch strips across the width of fabric

From EACH of the fabrics – green, yellow, blue swirls cut the following rectangles:
Five 2 ½ x 4 ½ inches
Five 2 ½ x 8 ½ inches
Nine 2 ½ x 12 ½ inches
And two 2 ½ inch strips across the width of fabric

Keep any left-over fabrics.

Celtic Eternity

Sewing

Use a ¼ inch seam allowance and press seams as you go

Block 1- Celtic knot blocks
Sew a yellow 2 ½ x 12 ½ inch strip to the top of a black 12 ½ inch square. Sew a blue swirls 2 ½ x 12 ½ inch strip to the bottom of the 12 ½ inch black square.

To each end of a green and a blue 2 ½ x 12 ½ inch strip, sew a black 2 ½ inch square.
Sew the green strip to the right hand side of the black 12 ½ inch square. Sew the blue to the left hand side of the black 12 ½ inch square.

Make 4 of these blocks and put to one side until you are ready to apply the Celtic applique

Block 2 -Chain blocks

Sew a 2 ½ x 4 ½ inch yellow strip to the top of a 4 ½ inch square
Sew a 2 ½ x 4 ½ inch blue swirls strip to the bottom of the 4 ½ inch square
To each end of a green and blue 2 ½ x 4 ½ inch strip, sew a black 2 ½ inch square.
Sew the blue strip to the left hand side of the black 4 ½ inch square. Sew the green to the right hand side of the black 4 ½ inch square.

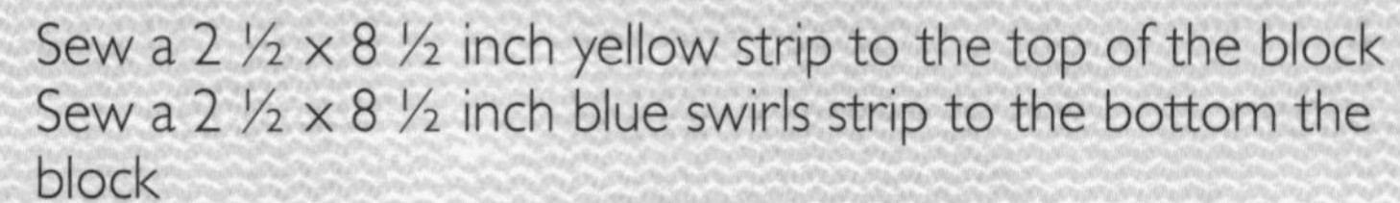

Sew a 2 ½ x 8 ½ inch yellow strip to the top of the block
Sew a 2 ½ x 8 ½ inch blue swirls strip to the bottom the block
To each end of a green and blue 2 ½ x 8½ inch strip, sew a black 2 ½ inch square.
Sew the blue to the left hand side of the block. Sew the green strip to the right hand side of the block.

Sew a 2 ½ x 12 ½ inch yellow strip to the top of the block
Sew a 2 ½ x 12 ½ inch blue swirls strip to the bottom the block
To each end of a green and a blue 2 ½ x 12½ inch strip, sew a black 2 ½ inch square.
Sew the blue strip to the left hand side of the block. Sew the green strip to the right hand side of the block.

Celtic Knot Applique

Please note the Celtic knots are made form 2 different colours. 2 blue and 2 green.
You will need approx. 90 inches of ¼ inch bias tape for each Celtic knot. You can buy ready-made fusible bias, this is the easiest option.
If you wish to make your own you will need a bias making tool. Follow instructions to make ¼ inch bias tape. You will have enough fabric left over if you wish to make your own.
Trace the Celtic knot (found on templates page 50) onto tracing paper with an iron-on transfer pencil. Centre and Place the tracing paper on your block- transfer side down, and use an iron on the wool setting to transfer the design onto your fabric. Work slowly and check to see if the design is transferring.

Start with the end of the bias tape on a intersection. Chose an under, so the raw edge will be covered when you cross back over it. Follow the design. Carefully note the location of the intersections, and whether the tape is to go under or over. Pin the bias tape to the background fabric. If you have fusible bias you can iron it in place as you go.

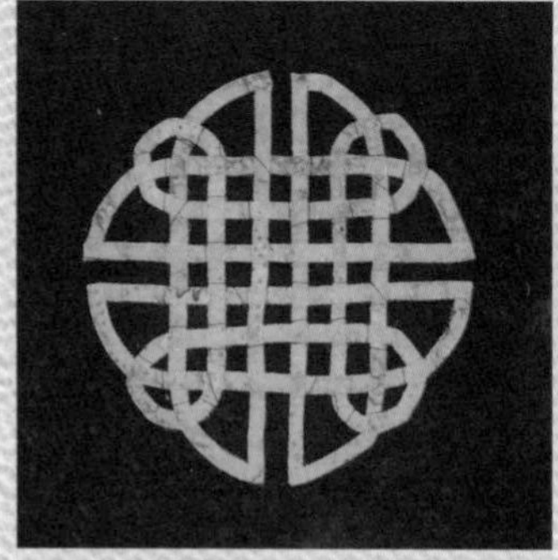

Use a invisible thread, or a matching thread.
Stitch down the fused bias tape. Sew a straight line down each side of the tape, turning the block slowly and smoothly on the curves. You can also use a decorative stitch, such as a blanket or zigzag stitch. You can also use twin needles; refer to your sewing machine manual for further details.

As you complete your design, you can tuck the last piece which will meet the start, under the strip of bias that crosses over.

Complete all four Celtic knot applique blocks.

Refer to the picture, to layout the blocks. Keep all the chain blocks facing the same way.
Sew the blocks together in rows, sew the rows together.

Adding Borders

Refer to the picture for border placement. There is a different colour border strip on each side.

Join two yellow 2 ½ inch strips together. Cut to 48 ½ and sew to the top of the quilt. Refer to the picture for placement
Join two blue swirls strips together 2 ½ inch strips. Cut to 48 ½ and sew to the bottom of the quilt. Refer to the picture for placement
Join two green 2 ½ inch strips together. Cut to 48 ½ inches. Sew a black square to each end of the strip and sew onto the right hand side of the quilt . Refer to the picture for placement.
Join two blue 2 ½ inch strips together. Cut to 48 ½ inches. Sew a black 2 ½ inch square to each end of the strip and sew to the left hand side of the quilt. Refer to the picture for placement

Outer border

Join together six 2 ½ inch black strips into a continuous length.
From this length cut two borders 52 ½ inches long. Sew to either side of the quilt
Cut another two borders 56 ½ inches long sew to the top and bottom of the quilt.

Join the remaining 2 ½ inch strips into a continuous length for the binding and follow instructions on page 45 for finishing instructions.

Celtic Swirls

Celtic inspired with that mystical feel

Celtic Swirl

Finished size 13 x 34 inches

You can customise any pattern or item with some Celtic inspired applique to give it that mystical feel. Here I have used some of my favourite colours and fabric to make a table runner. It can be made in any measurement to fit any table. It would also look great as a wall hanging.

Requirements:

You can work with any colour group. Pick a dark, dramatic fabric for the main fabric. This will really make the other colours stand out. Using silks also adds something really special, and it doesn't have to be costly, you can pick up cheaper silks off the internet, or at a market.

- A foundation fabric such as muslin or calico 36 x 14 inchs
- 4/5 fat eighths (11x18 inches)
- 18 inches of a dark batik or similar
- 10 inches of a contrasting colourful fabric
- 3 inch strip from a different dark fabric
- 5 inch strip of fusible webbing
- Wadding and backing to fit

Cutting:

From the selection of fat 1/8 cut approx:
Twenty pieces all 3 ½ inches wide varying sizes between 1 ½ and 2 ½ inches

From the dark batik fabric cut:
Three 2 ½ inch strips across the width of fabric (binding)
One strip 2 ½ x 36 inches

From the second dark fabric cut:
One strip 2 ½ x 36 inches

From the bright contrasting fabric cut:
Two 5 x 36 inch strips

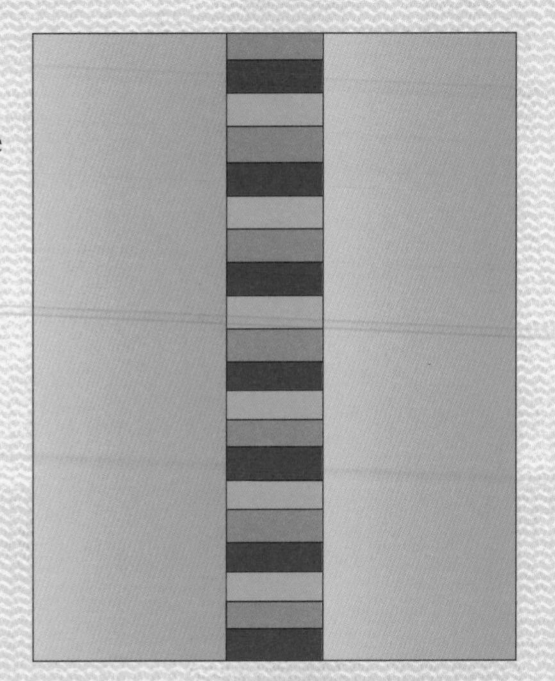

Sewing

Sew all the pieces together measuring 3 ½ inch wide into one long piece, sew them in a random order, the final length should be 36 inches.

Place onto the centre of the foundation fabric lengthways, pin in place
Lay the 5 inch contrasting fabric strips either side of the centre panel, so the raw edges are butted against each other. Pin in place.

Cut the first dark batik strip measuring 2 ½ x 36 in half lengthways using a wavy line. Repeat with the second dark fabric. Lay the strips on top of the table runner. Pin in place. Refer to the photograph for reference.

Quilt as you go

Layer up with wadding and backing. Pin and tack layers together refer to page 45 for finishing instructions.
Quilting suggestion - Quilt along the dark fabrics, meander with the walking foot and a straight stitch to create wavy lines. You will need to quilt approx. 1 inch apart, to hold the fabric layers down. Keep the quilting on the dark fabrics only.

On the paper side of fusible webbing trace 3 large spirals and 1 small spiral. Cut each one out roughly. Iron onto the reverse of your chosen fabrics. Cut out on the drawn line, remove the paper backing. Place the spirals onto the table runner. When you are happy with the placement iron in place to fuse. Use a decorative stitch, or zig zag on your machine to applique the spirals.
Square and trim to 34 x 13 inches

Join the binding strips together and follow the finishing instructions on page 46.

Finishing

Prepare your quilt for quilting - Ensure your wadding and backing are slightly larger than the finished quilt top. Give the backing a press with a hot dry iron do not stretch the fabric when ironing; Place the backing fabric on a flat surface, right side down. Place the wadding on top of the backing, smooth out layers and make sure there are no wrinkles in the fabric or wadding. Place the quilt on top of the wadding right side up; make sure the wadding and backing are showing around all the edges. Smooth out the top and check the backing and wadding are still flat. Secure with pins starting from the middle working outwards. Check the layers are still flat as you continue to pin. Now tack all the layers together, using a running stitch - vertically and horizontally.

Quilting:
You are now ready. There are so many different ways you can quilt it is difficult to know where to start. Quilt to your level and ability. If you are a beginner then it is a good idea to just do the minimum of quilting. As you progress with new projects, your quilting skills will also progress.

Hand Quilting:
Use a rocking or stab stitch to hold the layers together. You can do a little or a lot depending on time, skill and patience.

Machine Quilting:
You will need a walking foot for your machine, and again you can quilt as little or as much as you want. It can be difficult with a large quilt to get it through the arm of your machine, but if you take your time it is do-able.

Free Motion Machine Quilting:
You will need a special foot, this is like a darning foot. You will need to drop the feed dogs or use a flat plate over the feed dogs depending on the make of your machine. You have more freedom over where you stitch and you do not need to turn the quilt so much. This is useful when working with a large quilt. Also you can create patterns that would be impossible to do with the walking foot. However it does take a certain amount of skill and confidence.

Tying:
If you feel daunted or are always put off by quilting then you can tie your quilt. Using a heavy weight thread, make a stitch through the three layers leaving the thread on top, go through the stitch twice leaving the end thread on top. Tie the two ends together, leave ends loose as decoration.

Buttons:
You can also tie your quilt together using buttons. If you wish you can use a combination of the above methods.

There is also long arm quilting- this is a great idea for a special quilt. You give it to a professional with a specialist machine. You choose or decide a pattern for your quilt, and leave it with the quilter. The beauty of this is you do not have to layer it up; the quilter will do that for you and is included in the price.

Nikki at work on her Janome Horizon sewing machine

Binding:
Prepare the binding to the right length. This will be the width x 2 and the length x 2 , plus 6 extra inches. Join continuous lengths of 2 ½ inch wide strips until you get to this measurement. Join the strips on the diagonal as in diagram A.

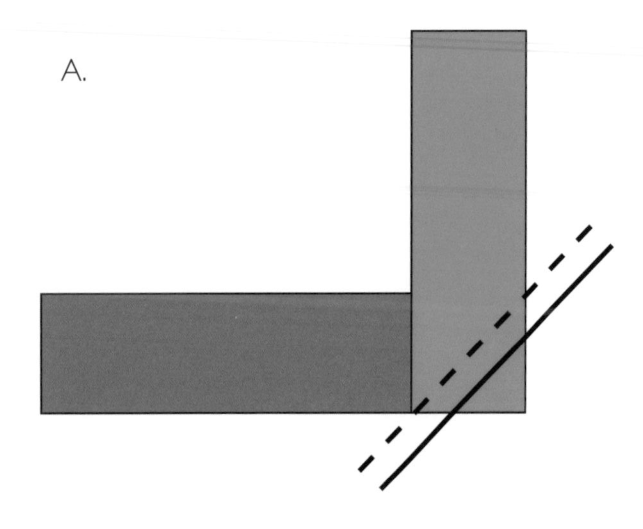

Place fabrics face to face. The dotted line indicates the sewing line, and the solid line indicates the cutting line.

Press the prepared binding in half lengthways, wrong sides together.

Leave a tail of six inches and start in the middle on one side of the quilt; align raw edges with the edge of quilt. Sew through all layers with a ¼ inch seam allowance. Stop a ¼ inch from the corner, fold the binding up and then down to create a triangle of fabric (see diagram B). This is a mitred corner.

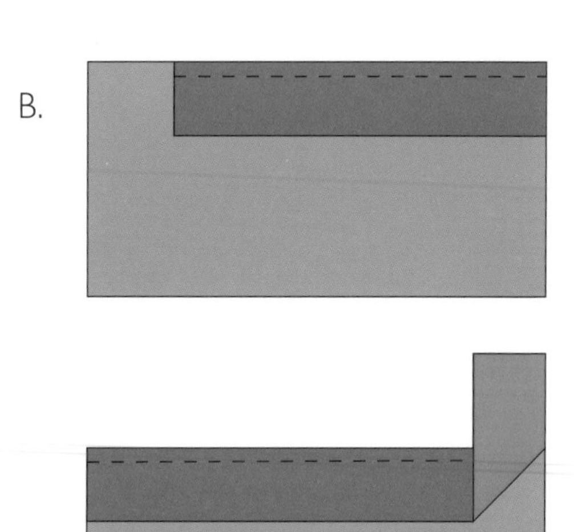

Turn and start a ¼ inch down and continue sewing the next side. Repeat the mitred corners.
Continue sewing and stop approx 5 inches from the starting point. Remove from the machine and cut the thread.

To join the binding for finishing : Fold both pieces so they meet on a 45 deg angle and finger crease. Lift away from the quilt and pin the two pieces of binding together aligning the crease on each piece. Sew on the crease line. Trim a ¼ inch away from the stitch line. Place back down onto the quilt (see diagram C).
Turn binding to the back and hand stitch in place.

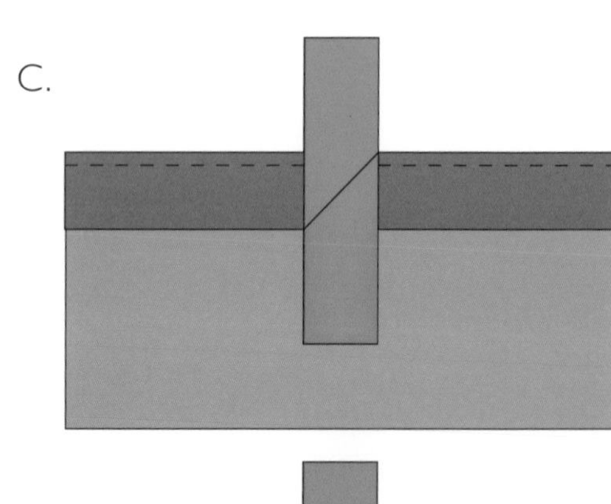

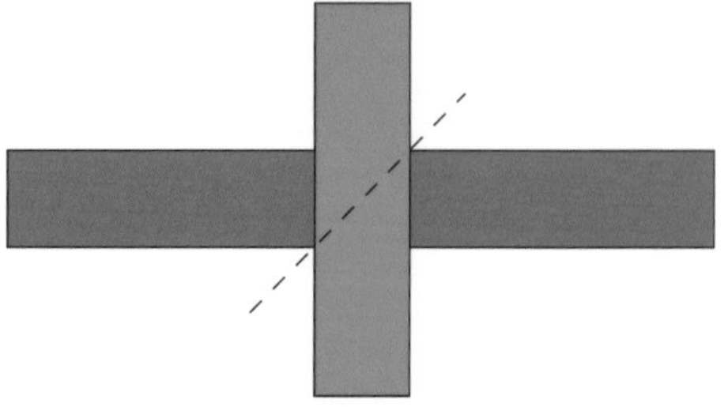

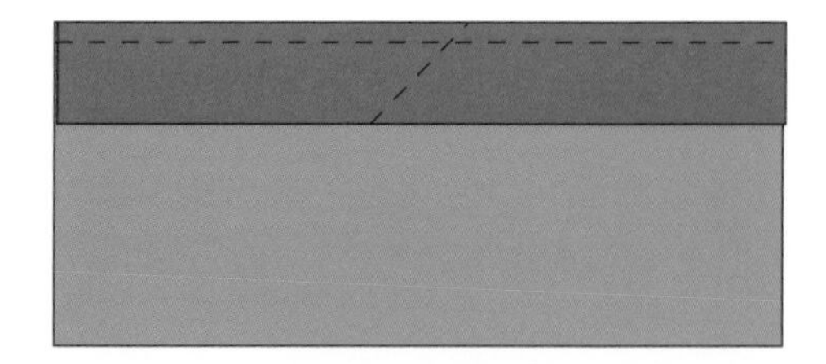

Dying Fabric in Bags

Dying your own fabric is fun, with great results. Here is a very basic method how to dye your own fabrics. When you have tried this method then you can experiment a bit more. I use reactive dyes; they have the salt already added in, but check when you purchase your dyes. You may need to add salt. Read all instructions first that come with your dyes, including the safety instructions.

You Will Need:

- Waterproof Gloves
- Plastic teaspoons
- 20 Strong plastic bags, (large zip bags)
- 6/8 Jars, not too small. Or a jar for each colour (A few spares in case you want to mix your own colours)
- 1 Medium Sized Bucket
- 4 /5 yards of plain white cotton/ Dyers cotton/(Commercial tone on tone also works well)
- Washing Soda
- Reactive craft dyes. (procion reactive)

Read the instructions for the particular dye you are using.

Method:

Cut your fabric into fat quarters, or similar manageable sizes. Place a cup of washing soda into a plastic bucket and fill with lukewarm water. Stir with a wooden spoon until the washing soda is dissolved, place in the cut fabric. Leave for at least one hour (even better if you can leave it over night) Lift out the fabric and wring out as much as possible to remove excess liquid.

The next bit is trial and error for the first time; you will still get great results. Have one jar and one plastic teaspoon for each colour of dye. Fill each jar with two/three inches of lukewarm water. Add approx one level teaspoon of dye to each jar. Mix thoroughly until dye has dissolved. Keep each teaspoon with the correct colour.

Photographs on this page courtesy of Sarah Noonan

PLEASE NOTE:
INCREASE AMOUNT OF DYE FOR YELLOW AND REDUCE AMOUNT FOR TURQUOISE

Place a piece of fabric in each bag, start with 8 bags. Using the teaspoons add the liquid dye to the fabric. Add one colour at a time; try mixing the colours in the bags. Don't over mix the colours. i.e. Add red, then yellow **or** blue/red.

Experiment; try using colour groups, such as opposites, or colours next to each other on the colour wheel. Make sure that the fabric is saturated with dye; agitate the fabric in the bag to ensure the fabric absorbs the dye. Try doing it with one colour- agitate, add another colour-don't agitate. This will give you a space dyed effect. If you have one colour that you particularly like you can add another piece of fabric to the bag and agitate. The second piece will be a lighter version of the first one.

The colours should look vibrant in the bags. Continue till all the fabric and dye is used up. Try to work within the hour as the dye starts to lose strength after that. If for example you had a drop of yellow dye left over, you could tip it into a bag of fabric already dyed with that colour. Leave the fabric in the bags overnight, then rinse out the fabric in cold water until the water runs clear. Squeeze out and hang to dry, whilst still damp ,iron dry.

Terminology

There can be a lot of terminology in sewing books. It's hard to follow a pattern if you have no idea what some of the instructions mean.

Here are some of the things you may come across:

Width of fabric:
'... cut four strips 2 ½ inch wide across the width of fabric' – this may also be written as
'... cut four strips 2 ½ inch wide across WOF.

The width of the fabric or WOF is referring to the fabric from edge to edge as it comes off the roll. From selvage to selvage. (See next)

Selvage:
A tightly woven edge that runs along both outer edges of a fabric's length. Selvage edges keep the fabric from fraying. Sometimes it has information on such as the fabric designer or company that printed it, it runs along the edge of the fabric as it comes off the roll.

Block Measurements:
When referring to block size:
The finished size is the size your block or border will be when it is stitched into your quilt. It does not include seam allowance. So take care when reading instructions if a block states the finished size is 10 x 10 inches, then the size before you sew it into your quilt will be 10 ½ x 10 ½ .The extra ½ allows for the seam allowance of ¼ inch on both sides.
This can cause great confusion if you do not understand it

Fat Quarter:
This is a name for a ¼ yard piece of fabric cut in a square instead of a strip.
The measurement of a fat quarter is 18x22 inches. Four squares of this measurement put together make one yard.

Fat Eighth:
A fat eighth is a fat quarter cut in half.
The measurement of a fat eight is 9 x 11 inches.

Template 01

Template 02 (template shown at 85% of actual size)

Template 03

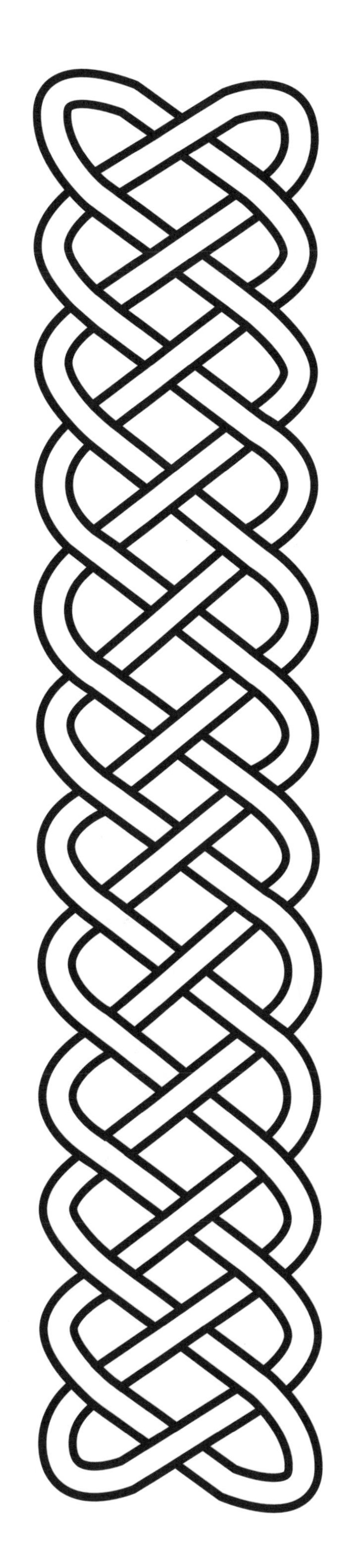

Cú Chulain's Love Throw

Template 04

Template 05

Cú Chulain's Love Throw

Template 06 (template shown at 85% of actual size)

Template 07

Template 08

Template 09

Shamrocks & St. Patrick's Day Mug Mats

Template 10

Patchwork Fields are Green

Template 11

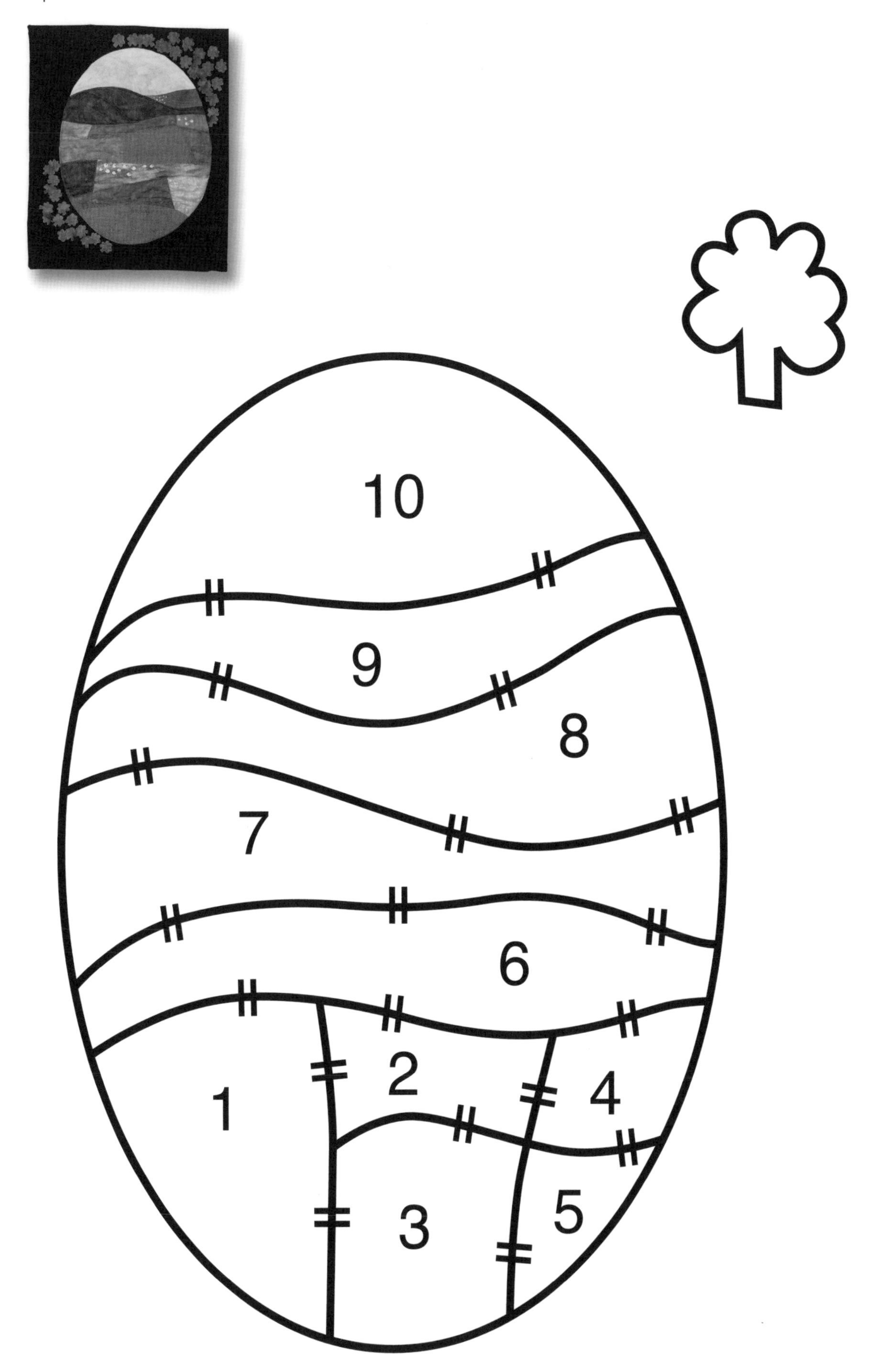